SPEAK LIKE A PRO

SPEAK LIKE A PRO

Terry Paulson, PhD, CSP, CPAE

Amber Eagle Press
Agoura Hills, CA

Speak Like a Pro
© 2013 by Terry L. Paulson
ISBN: 978-1-878077-27-1 (paperback)
ISBN: 978-1-878077-26-4 (Kindle)
ISBN: 978-1-878077-25-7 (eBook)

Amber Eagle Press
28717 Colina Vista
Agoura Hills, CA 91301
terry@terrypaulson.com
www.terrypaulson.com

Some material from this book was included in 50 *Tips for Speaking Like a Pro*, Crisp
Publications, Inc., printing, 1999. Printed in the United States of America

CONTENTS

INTRODUCTION

"I do not object to people looking at their watches when I am speaking – but I strongly object when they start shaking them to make certain they are still going."

— Lord Birkett

"With less time on their hands, executives wind up putting off writing their speeches until the last minute – which means doing it while en route to their destination. Of the 400 executives of leading U.S. companies, 44% write their speeches on the plane for out-of-town meetings. Twenty-eight percent wrote their speeches in the office before leaving. And 14% did their writing in the hotel room before they went on stage. None of the executives confirmed he or she would rather die than give a speech. But 20% would rather do income taxes and another 20% would rather try to lose 10 pounds in a month. Fifteen percent would rather have a cavity filled."

— Michael Klepper

"Deliver each speech like it is your last, and treat the audience like it is their first!"

— Shep Hyken, CPAE, CSP

I know what you might be saying: "What a nice thought, but I'm afraid my first and last speeches are going to be the same one and the audience will applaud that news!" We've all been there with you. You've been asked to give a presentation, and as the event approaches, panic starts to set in. Your fear: an audience of stone-faced zombies sitting motionless while you stumble through the worst 15 minutes of your life. This dreadful mental picture is common among inexperienced speakers. It reminds me of my start in speaking as a church youth leader. After all, when you speak to teens, you have to be funny and authentic or they kill you. Don't worry, help is on the way!

This book consists of time-tested "how to" tips and practical suggestions that I've learned the hard way along with the insights from some of the best speakers in the world. Whether you are a new speaker, an executive required to speak, or an experienced professional, taking the time to read and explore these windows to excellence in speaking will help you on your own journey to become a more effective speaker. For many, the insights will be fresh. For experienced speakers, the content and quotes will challenge you to take a fresh look at your speaking autopilot. Even the best must continue to refresh and retool their skills and their passion for speaking. The tips have been assembled in a sequence helping you find the information you need. We start by helping you prepare to speak. There is a section on delivery, and one on what to do after you have finished to benefit from your experience. If you are struggling with one specific area, you can quickly get to it with the topical headings. For those who value lifelong learning, take one tip a week and focus on it in depth. With focused execution, you may even give yourself a couple of weeks off for good behavior.

Some of the insights listed in this book first appeared in a prior book published by Crisp Publications and Course Technology, a division of Thomson Learning. I want to personally thank the many professionals, coaches and writers who shared their insights and quotes. Whether they knew it or not, each has been a mental mentor for my own career. I never stand in awe of the best; I try to learn from each of them.

I have had the privilege of being president of both the National Speakers Association and the Global Speakers Federation. These professional associations have provided both a nurturing network and a consistent source for stimulating training. They've been incubators for my career and for the careers of many other top professional speakers. In fact, if you apply some of the speaking tips in this book, you may become good enough that people call you back for an encore, and this time ask you to speak *for pay*. If that starts to happen frequently, do yourself a favor and join NSA and GSF, the voices for the speaking industry here in America and around the world. By doing so, you *will accelerate* your speaking career and inherit a family of speakers that are ready to support you doing just that. Get more information on both organizations and their local chapters at nsaspeaker.org and globalspeakers.net.

No matter what you learn from your experience or this book, never stop growing as speaker. Don't let audiences convince you that you have "arrived." What they say to you at the front of the room may not match what they say behind your back. Cavett Robert, the founder of NSA, used to say, "The only reliable readings are restroom readings – go into your stall early and really listen to what people have to say." That's good advice for all of us. Make sure you cultivate mentors that *care enough* to give you honest feedback eyeball to eyeball. I've always appreciated the wise counsel of my great uncle from the farms of Illinois who used to say, "If one person calls you a horse's ass, don't worry. If four people do, go out and buy a saddle." in short, let's all take the time to keep listening and keep learning, and spending a little more time in the restroom.

Remember the perspective Winston Churchill tried to keep. When a chairwoman at a presentation said to Churchill, "Doesn't it thrill you, Mr. Churchill, to see all those people out there who came just to see you?" Churchill answered, "It is quite flattering, but whenever I feel this way I always remember that if instead of making a political speech I was being hanged, the crowd would be twice as big."

Now, expecting a more positive outcome to your next presentation, get busy soaring on the wings of words and taking your audiences with you!

In Support,

Terry L. Paulson, PhD, CSP, CPAE

THE POWER OF PURPOSE

"We are not the stars – our audience is. We are not the center of attention – the message is."

— Connie Podesta, CSP, MS, LPC

Know your "why" before you even consider the "how." The Indians have a saying to describe speakers who say too little too loudly – "High wind, big thunder, no rain." If there is no core, no vital need being met, no life being changed, no dream being planted and nurtured, no strategic impact to the meeting, why speak? A presentation without at least a seed of insight, help, hope, or inspiration is a hallow imitation of the noble art of oratory. The right to speak is a precious privilege. As such, the speaker had better prepare himself to be a medium for amazement and impact.

You may speak often, but every presentation is opening night for your audience. Keep centered on your purpose by helping instead of just persuading. You are leading your audience on a treasure hunt to the value of your message. You may want to borrow my prayer that helps me tap the power of purpose before every speech: "Lord, help me to serve not just to shine; help me empower not just impress." As a professional speaker, I've learned that when you serve your audience, you will be remembered, repeated, referred and rehired long after any standing ovation is forgotten. As Bill Gove, CSP, CPAE confided, "Just before I speak, I say to myself – 'In a few seconds I will be doing what I love to do in front of some people who really want me to do well. I can hardly wait to get out there, because that is where I belong!'"

As a leader facing an important speech, never lose sight of your organization's mission and vision. There is power that comes with a message focused on strategic progress. By asking yourself how your presentation helps others invent a desired future, you focus more on impact than on just making a good impression.

Your sense of purpose will also keep you humble after your great speeches and warm during the tough times. Keep cheating yesterday's audience by doing a better job each time you speak. May a spirit of thankfulness take you beyond the job of speaking to the calling it can be. For centuries, speakers have made a lasting difference. Now, it is your turn to do the same.

HAVE PASSION FOR YOUR TOPIC

"Forget all the conventional 'rules' but one. There is one golden rule: Stick to topics you deeply care about and don't keep your passion buttoned inside your vest. An audience's biggest turn-on is the speaker's obvious enthusiasm. If you are lukewarm about the issue, forget it!"

— Tom Peters

To grab an audience make sure there is a light at your core. There is a certain zest that shines through a presenter's face when they speak of something they have authentic passion for. That speaker can be excited and whisper, and it still gets through. Don't just speak on any subject; speak on ones you live! What do you believe in enough that no one can stop you from finding a place to share it? When you have passion for your message, you'll feel like saying, "Get over here now! You don't want to miss this!" in such a talk, your hour of speaking feels like minutes. Great speakers don't just love to speak; they love to make a difference for people. Finish this sentence: "I love speaking; I get to . . . " If you ever struggle to find the motivation and the enthusiasm to start your speech, take a moment to go back to your success history as a speaker to review images you have retained that affirm what your presentations have meant to past audiences. Relive that image before you take to the platform. Feed your own enthusiasm for your message as you get ready to make a difference again.

As a leader who does not always get to pick the topics you speak on, don't take lightly the challenge of building your own enthusiasm. If you struggle, talk to those who do. Ask them to explain: Why is this important? How does this fit into our strategic plan? What do you hope to come from this message? Let them know you want to do the presentation justice.

After all, if you have no enthusiasm for your message, why should anyone else? Find the passion in your purpose, or find another topic to speak on or another person to deliver the message.

RELEVANCE MATTERS

"I like to keep everything substantive, short and to the point. I always shoot for take-home value. If I were sitting out there myself in the audience, what would I want to hear that I could write down and use the next morning."

— Harvey Mackay, CPAE

Stay focused on what adds value! Remember, a good presentation needs to be more about the audience and less about you. It's important to have a message you believe in, but make sure it is one your audience needs to hear. Making an impact as a speaker requires stimulating a need, piquing curiosity and creating a motivation to want to acquire what you have to say.

You don't have to entertain me; show me its relevance to my career, my life or my paycheck, and I challenge you to bore me. Take the time before any program to make sure you are in synch with your audience. A great message at the wrong time or with the wrong audience will not generate enthusiasm or the desired outcomes. Be flexible and have a thorough grasp of ways you can control your program mix to play to your audience.

Most learning will come in the areas your audience is living. Hit them there to generate authentic excitement. Do you know the challenges, obstacles and opportunities your audience is living now? If not, start asking a few questions and listen for the content that can guide your preparation. Whatever you do, make sure your message fits their world.

DEFINE THE MISSION
FOR YOUR MESSAGE
IN A SENTENCE

"People don't listen to marketplace logic; they listen for meaning and purpose. Attention can't be bought. Before any interaction, ask yourself: 'How do I want to make people feel or act?' Put yourself in their shoes. The role of a leader is to create an experience that will inspire people to take action."

— Bill Jensen

Movie producers want scriptwriters to know their "high concept" – the one phrase or sentence that defines what the movie is about. You've asked people who have seen a movie that age old question, "What was it about?" A speech can often last slightly less than a movie. Try some of these questions on for size as you prepare for your talk: If your audience would have to describe what you said, what would you want them to say? If a reporter was in your audience and made a headline, what would you want it to read? Why is what you are saying going to make a difference to the people hearing you? If you had to explain the value of your talk in an elevator ride, what would you say to get them excited about attending? If you had one sentence rather than 45 minutes, what would you say?

With all these questions in mind, write down your mission or objective in one simple paragraph that identifies the audience's primary needs and how you will meet them. Keep it where you can see it as you prepare your message and ensure take-home value to the people attending your presentation. Use it as a tool that helps you include or reject content and stories in your presentation. Just because you love a story or a statistic doesn't mean that it belongs in particular presentation. When your mission is clear, decision making will be much easier.

YOUR UNIQUENESS

"Be yourself . . . but even more so."

— Patricia Fripp, CSP, CPAE

The biggest enemy of any speaker is sameness. There's a temptation for beginning speakers to protect themselves by trying to be somebody else while presenting. When this happens to you, your message will come across as shallow and sterile.

Elbert Hubbard said it well, "The great orators are inspired by many but copies of none." Your greatest power on the platform will always come from your natural talents and your strongest beliefs and opinions. By not letting them see what you have to offer you cheat your audience. Accept the risk that comes with being truly authentic; it is the only place you can find your own unique power and value.

Once you find your unique voice, keep refining it. What issues or topics can channel your expertise, your heart and your life experience? If you need more help to discover it, identify six to ten of the most significant or memorable events in your life on and off the job. Explore what unique lessons they carry for others.

You will always be the expert in what works for you – your unique window to what works in the great game of life. Be a translator of that experience to others. When you let go of trying to be a "me too" speaker, you have a chance of becoming a truly great presenter. As John Mason once said, "You were born an original. Don't die a copy."

ETHICS BUILDS CRITICAL TRUST

"Leadership is really to do with getting people to follow you to a place you haven't been, which is the future. It has to do with change. People won't willingly follow someone into the unknown unless they can trust that person's instincts and values. . . . In the middle of change, you have to have some things that don't change, which are strong values."

— Sidney Taurel

Be a presenter who "walks his talk." In spite of what media surveys may suggest, maintaining integrity is always important in gaining trust and in getting a message across. Even more important, honor is a gift you give yourself *and* your audiences. People watch you as you talk to people before you speak. They note how you do business and how you respond to problems before and after your talk. They want to see how you behave in the hallways when the lights are down and the microphone is off. Perfect people exist only in educational movies, but you can aspire to be congruent on and off the platform. If an audience smells a rat, they most certainly won't buy your message. As speaker Sheila Murray Bethel likes to warn, "Don't get caught with your ethics down."

For leaders, trust is a fragile commodity that is important to maintain, easy to lose, and hard to win back. If you don't talk about and act on your values, don't expect those who work with you to trust your messages. In his book, *Credibility*, Tom Peters maintains that trustworthiness and believability are the foundation of all leadership and influence. If it is true that "the best leaders work by principles, not rules," by centering on a commitment to organizational values, you can increase your influence every time you speak.

Mark Twain said it well, "Always do what is right. It will gratify most of the people, and astound the rest."

POWER COMES WITH
AN ASSERTIVE POINT OF VIEW

"When you're thinking about what you want to say, it is often helpful to distill the message, in your own mind, to a sentence or two. If you can't quite see the sentence in your mind, try to imagine a newspaper headline that reports the content of the speech."

— Peggy Noonan

Don't just be unique; be unique for a reason! You have your mission, but what is your unique point of view that speaks to that mission. Bottom-line your message on what people need to hear and act on. Impacting an audience as a leader means assertively communicating your point of view enhanced by supportive facts, relevant stories that reinforce your company's culture, appropriate humor, and impactful quotes.

Developing an assertive communication style is all about clarity with passion and openness. It's about using "I" statements and taking a stand. While making room for the opinions of others, be ready to constructively challenge opposing viewpoints. You'll want to use only the data, facts and graphs that make a difference. Give the appropriate level of detail. Be strategic instead of just tactical. You want your message to be supported by the data without getting stuck in information overload.

A point of view fired by personal conviction and commitment to its importance has an impact. So, why is what you're saying important for the audience to hear? An audience's biggest turn-on is the speaker's obvious enthusiasm for what they are sharing.

But it is more than enthusiasm; you'll find power in the conviction you have for sharing the right message at the right time. You want to challenge your audiences to learn more than they now know. Consider your information and the expertise you share as a value your audience needs. It's been said that no news is good news. On the contrary, no news is *no* news.

For most people, the failure to share relevant information, input or suggestions wastes resources and time. Sadly, the greatest gift you can give today's associate is often a canceled meeting! Don't let that be said about yours.

With a clear point of view, you'll soon start identifying what you have to prove it — your facts, graphs, humor, anecdotes, narratives, case histories, and quotes from experts.

USE ON-TARGET HUMOR

"All I'm trying to do is show where humor fits in. It's not a yuk-a-minute. It's not a bunch of jokes. It forces you to think about every point you're going to make during a speech. All (humor) does is reinforce traditional practices but in a more pleasant, fun kind of way . . . "

— Malcolm L. Kushner

Don't just leave humor to chance; find and craft on-target humor that increases the impact of your presentation. Use humor to provide pegs for retention, illustrate key points, provide meaningful commentary, relieve tension, or generate genuine enthusiasm and warmth in your audience.

Be ready to capitalize on the humor that naturally occurs. Look for opportunities to laugh over funny mistakes or a humorous coincidence or comment. Humor tends to relax and stimulate people and make them more receptive to the message at hand. So, instead of jokes, use humor that arises naturally from the context of who you are, where you are, and what you have to say. That is what "wit" is all about – it is more important to have fun presenting than to be funny.

Knowing that you have limited time, look for and use humor that enhances the content and purpose of your talk. Before using humor, don't just ask, "Is it funny?" Ask yourself: Does it work in getting my point across in a timely, tactful, and tasteful way? Does a humorous story provide meaningful commentary? Will it be a bonus that moves my message along? Remember, even a good funny story can't be substituted for a good information and sound support information that helps accomplish your mission.

"But my presentation is serious," you might say. Aram Bakshian, Jr. reminds us, "People want to laugh. Even in serious talks humor comes as a relief – it can defuse tough situations, unite an audience and really bond you to an audience."

For people to relate, the setting of any humorous story must create a familiar image in the mind's eye of the listener. That is why humor that relates to only one culture should be left out of presentations to international audiences. A good humorous anecdote or story from your work or from home can prompt the listener to say, "I can see it happening!" "I've been there!" or "It could happen to me!" When they connect your story with their life's experience, they retain your story and your point whenever they think of their own similar experiences.

Use only relevant humor. Think of the roles you have had that relate to the content of your presentation and try to remember humorous incidents that have occurred in those roles. Also begin collecting humorous content in one of your email folders. At the end of the day, look through the "eye of the loon" for anything funny that occurred. Document it in an email and send it to yourself to save for some future presentation when it just may provide the perfect humorous illustration.

HAVE A HUMOR CODE

"When someone blushes with embarrassment . . . , when someone carries away an ache . . . , when something sacred is made to appear common . . . , when someone's weakness provides the laughter . . . , when profanity is required to make it funny . . . , when a child is brought to tears . . . , or when everyone can't join in the laughter . . . , it's a poor joke!"

— Cliff Thomas

Not all humor works in speaking. Know the difference between "helping" and "hurting" humor. Laughing *with* others doesn't reinforce stereotypes or single any group out for ridicule. On the contrary, such humor pulls all together as we laugh at universal human foibles. Instead of bringing people together, sarcastic humor and ethnic or gender jokes tend to keep people apart. If you must use ethnic, gender or regional humor, make it at the expense of your own ethnic group, your own gender, or your own region.

Getting a laugh is never worth putting down any other group. Offended listeners seldom appreciate even your good ideas. A comedian asks, "Is it funny?" A good speaker asks a different question, "Does my humor work to enhance the impact, clarity or retention of my intended message?" For a handy rule of thumb: If what you say might offend someone, leave it out!

SHARE STRIKING STORIES

"The best speakers illustrate their talks with short, striking vignettes. In fact, the most potent speeches are often little more than strings of such vignettes, loosely linked by an outline."

— Tom Peters

Story is what penetrates. People remember *and* speakers remember narrative "chunks" more easily than they ever remember specific content or abstract teaching points. Good stories unlock those seldom used doors that lead the listener through their own house of memories. Those memories, once triggered, allow audiences to experience themselves, their lives on and off the job, and their memories in a fresh way.

Good stories will help you as a speaker organize your content around your stories. If you do, you will seldom need notes to keep you on track. Having a story to illustrate all of your main points will save you if your PowerPoint computer or projector ever malfunctions. After all, a good organized storyteller can always make a point, tell a story . . . make a point, tell a story . . . and continue until their talk is over.

If you speak too fast with too many words you can be a menace, because you give people no time to think and connect to their own lives. Let each member of your audience enjoy his own train of thought and experiences. Consider it a compliment when someone says, "You are great speaker; you interrupted my train of thought 12 times."

At the same time, you want them to say, "What a great story worth remembering!" not just "What a great storyteller!" Afraid you won't have enough content or data? When was the last data slide or graph that you remember as a highlight of a talk. Make sure your story is supported by the facts, but use stories as a valuable tool in communicating your message.

A story's value must be worth the investment of time in sharing it. Few audiences can resist a good story, but when you have a brief time to impact an audience, you must edit for brevity and impact. While sharing a series of graphs and critical content, try playing your version of Paul Harvey – "Let me tell you 'the rest of the story.'" How can you help them understand the story behind the facts you are sharing? You're looking for what real people did or said that reinforces and enlivens your point of view and valuable information.

Hollywood story structure expert Robert McKee writes: "Stories are the creative conversion of life itself into a more powerful, clearer, more meaningful experience. They are the currency of human contact." We pay to go to movies, so try using the Hollywood model of character, dialogue and dramatic lesson to guide the crafting of shared anecdotes. In business presentations, use short, striking vignettes. They don't have to be heroic, but they need to be real and relevant. What short stories or anecdotes do you already like to share to highlight some of your most important life lessons?

FINDING AND USING
YOUR OWN STORIES

"The one thing I can give my audiences that no one else can give them is ME. My willingness to open up and let them in to the stories of my life makes all the difference in my programs."

— Barbara A. Mintzer

Still struggling to find your stories? You may want to try telling a story by engaging in role-play, to convey a specific message. For example, to make a point on the importance of honesty – When a neighbor came along to attend a movie with your family, he suggested that one of his boys could pass as younger and receive a discount. He said, "After all, who will know?" The father replied to the neighbor, "He will know." So you can start with interesting characters people can relate to; add sparkling dialogue that you bring to life; and end with an important lesson learned.

Remember, the best speakers use on-target stories from their own lives, their own industry or their own company to make their messages memorable. The best stories select you. They leap out at you and tell you that they will work. Think of how the message you are sharing impacted others: "Let me tell you about how enthusiastic . . . was when I told him . . . "

There are added advantages to using your own life experiences; your own stories are easy to remember and will be new to every audience. If you have a life, you have true stories to speak about. But the challenge is how to remember them.

Want to find your stories? Start by listing the places you have lived since childhood. Include as much detail as you can: Who lived there? Identify the secret places, the people you lived with, your friends, weird people, and the jobs you had. List the roles you played in each location. As a teen, I would list son, football player, Baskin Robbins "Scooper of the Month, youth leader, medal-winning quarter miler . . .

The more you write, the more you will see and hear in your mind's eye things you haven't thought of in years. Recreate your world and then start writing down all the unedited stories that emerge from your journey. Don't make entries long. Write a little, daydream a lot, write some more.

The best stories select you. They leap out at you and tell you that they will work because they are engaging, funny, or make a valuable point. Once found, practice telling your new stories to as many people as you can. Make your stories shorter and more impactful through practice. Save only those that have the most impact and move forward the messages you are called to speak on. Keep a list of your stories, keep adding to it, and review that list when you need to present.

TRUE STORIES?

"Never let the facts get in the way of a good story."

— Oscar Wilde

A good speaker embraces the audience and says you can be safe with me. Like a good actor, the facts and timeline of stories need not totally historically accurate, but it is important that stories be truthful to the essence of an experience. As a speaker you can emphasize certain statements and shape the story to support its emotional truth if it serves the audience. That is why we spend more time thinking about memories than we do looking at old videotapes.

After all, documentaries can take the fun out of remembering. Reporters tell facts; story tellers tell truths distilled through time to have impact today. Speakers don't show videos people don't want to see. They do tell stories that condense and enhance reality, create an emotional impact and reinforce important messages.

Stories aren't about facts, they're about experiences and turning points, yours and theirs. That's why the best professional speakers never take stories from other speakers. It's not only unethical; it's unwise. You will never be able to match their emotional connection to the experience they had. If you feel compelled to use the story of another, don't pretend that it is yours. Be honest — "Here's a story that was told to me by . . . It makes such a great point that I wanted to share it with you." But never forget that you will find your true uniqueness and power when you craft your own best stories for impact.

FIND AND WORK IN NEW MATERIAL

*"I'll come across a revealing quote in a business periodical . . .
or get asked a fascinating question at a seminar . . . or talk to
someone sitting next to me on a plane. Forty-eight hours later
. . . I'm using the slide in a seminar for 600 people, elaborat-
ing on the underlying story. Sometimes it falls flat. Sometimes
it begins to grow legs. If it sings, . . . I'll notice kindred stories.
Dig deeper into the original story. Make new slides. In a
handful of cases the seed-slide and its brothers and sisters becomes a completely new topic . . . I now know what I am, a
rapid prototyper! I have a passion for quickly turning a gleam
into a slide, a slide into a set of slides, etc. It's the way I
think."*

— Tom Peters

Develop an eye for new material wherever you go. When you see your
life as a journey in search of new content worth sharing, you will not only
find your own unique material, you will probably enjoy the journey more.
Renowned speaker Tom Peters made it a habit to include 15 minutes of
new material in each presentation. He would insert the new material between two strong segments. That way, even if it doesn't connect, the audience will think it was just pacing. By doing so, when he was ready to do an
"all new" presentation, each segment would have been tried on a live audience.

Working new material into every presentation you give will also keep
you fresh and growing. Besides impacting your audiences, personalizing and
adjusting your presentation content motivates the one person you can't get
away from — yourself! What are *you* doing to avoid the speaker *drone zone*
and keep your presentations and material fresh?

USING QUOTES AS
WINDOWS TO WISDOM

"What a good thing Adam had — when he said a good thing, he knew nobody had said it before him."

— Mark Twain

Use quotes from stakeholders and respected authorities to enhance the impact of your presentation. Being original is nice, but using the wisdom of others that has stood the test of time can be just as impressive to an audience. It honors both the person who said it and you. It also shows your audience that you can read and listen. A good quote can light up a room, unleash laughter, bring power or sudden depth to one of your points, and provide a memorable anchor that is remembered.

Hans Hofmann writes: "The ability to simplify means to eliminate the unnecessary so that the necessary may speak." By finding a simple but strong quote, you do just that. So, if a quote moves forward the objectives of your presentation, use it.

If you know your audience values a given authority, quote that authority in your message. Keep quotes and their sources for each of your topic areas in a searchable computer file. Don't be afraid to quote your own customers and associates or share quotes they provided to you. By doing so, you honor them.

The better you get at presenting, the more likely it is that they will be quoting you. You might even have fun by putting up a strong quote that you said from a previous presentation that people valued. When you read the quote, ask them, "Do you know who said this?" When no one replies, say, "I really wouldn't expect you to. It was me." They will laugh.

You can bring power to your quotes with advances in digital technology. Use a digital recorder and record a quote from an authority or member of the team. Take a picture and add both to a PowerPoint slide. Then your audience can both see and hear the person you are quoting. It brings variety to your presentation and true *power* to your PowerPoint.

In a world working to find the value of diversity in a global economy, do your part to find men and women of different backgrounds, cultures, and races so that you can honor the breadth of wisdom our diverse opinions can bring to any presentation. When you honor others, they may someday return the favor by quoting and honoring you.

GENUINENESS WORKS

"Audiences have seen smooth; they've seen slick. Don't fake who you are. When giving speeches, you can work so hard on the WHAT that you forget the WHO which is you. The audience wants to see your vulnerability and what you've done with your failures. They want you to offer hope that they too can overcome whatever obstacles come their way."

— Michael McKinley, CSP, CPAE

Being prepared does not mean being over-rehearsed. Too slick a performance breaks the emotional connection that must exist between a speaker and an audience for them to trust that the speaker really cares. The craft requires working and re-working the wording on certain stories, but they become practiced and rehearsed bits that are played by choice as a pianist would play a key on the piano. Each individual piano key is tuned, and in a great performance it is how they are played with passion and artistry that makes the difference.

The same is true with speaking. Hone the craft and then risk being real from the platform. Every mistake is endearing when handled well. That is the world the audience faces; they want you to face that world as well.

The only place that perfect people exist is in educational movies. They get to edit out their errors, and retake it until they get it right. In the real world, there are no dress rehearsals or retakes. You take it one day at a time by taking advantage of opportunities, overcoming obstacles, and making the best of your mistakes.

So don't be afraid to let a few of your mistakes show. After all, if they are too impressed with you, they may not believe that they are good enough to get the same results you have achieved. Be *real as a speaker* and you will *get real results.*

FRAME YOUR PRESENTATION INTO A STRUCTURE THAT WORKS

"The hard work is choosing, organizing, laying the foundation. You have the frame of the house. Now all you have to do is furnish it and flesh out each point."

— Peggy Noonan

Whether you're a Presidential speech writer or a budding but anxious amateur, you still need a structure for your speech. Cavett Robert, the founder of the National Speakers Association, used to say that every speech needs to have a front door, three rooms and a back door. Cavett would never add more rooms; he'd just add furniture to make the tour of that room last a little longer. If he faced time pressure, he could always stuff a few things in the closet and get through all three rooms in the time allotted.

The opening and closing are both critical. The audience wants to be sold on why they should even take time to come in. Once that choice is made, they don't want to waste much time getting inside to see what you have to offer. Show them the treasures you have prepared. People also want closure by having an ending that sounds like an ending and accomplishes the objectives established.

You may want to use a worksheet designed to build a sound presentation structure until it becomes second nature. Even then, the discipline of preparation will pay off in better, more focused presentations that produce the desired results.

PRESENTATION WORKSHEET

Topic: _____

Date: _____ Time: _____ Location: _____

Your audience needs:

Your purpose/objective/mission:

Your unique point of view:

Your close ("So in conclusion . . . "):

Your opening (Need, Story, Fact, Quote, or Question):

DEVELOP YOUR KEY POINTS:
Make a circle around each point. Use lines off each circle to note possible support material: research, quotes, stories/examples, humor, news items and key content as you think of them.

PREPARE BUT AVOID SCRIPTS

*"For heaven's sake, don't write it out! Careful preparation
spawns spontaneity. But it does mean never, ever writing it
out in full. If you do, you become a slave to your exact wording and inevitably lose 75 percent of any emotional impact."*

— Tom Peters

Preparation is important, but let's clarify the limits of preparation and
practice. Presenting means you have prepared enough to be spontaneous
and free while reciting is being over-prepared to the point that you are
trapped. Focus on what counts – make sure your major points get through.
You want them to know by your presentation that you've done the home-
work for them in finding the treasure from your window to the world.

Some call the preferred style "dialogue" presenting. Think of two people
talking across a kitchen table – it's comfortable, natural, and authentic. Rehearse; don't just practice. We too often overwork what we're going to say
in mental practice, but under work how we are going to say it.

Admittedly, some people are required to script out their entire message. When deviating from a script can result in a legal or political disaster, reading a script from a teleprompter makes sense. But most
presenters lose far more than they gain by preparing exact wording for an
entire speech. Craft and shape your openings and closings, but don't fall
victim to scripting the whole thing. As a pilot, you plan and execute with
precision your takeoff and landing, but they know once airborne how to
enjoy the ride taking people to the locations they want to see. Once you
are soaring on the wings of words, don't be trapped by the words you
have deposited on any page.

If you feel compelled to practice, vary your message. If you have no people to rehearse with, put Post-its® with smiley faces on chairs and speak to
the smile as you would people. Memorize your beginning and end, but
when you practice, practice with different words so you're not locked into
one way to deliver your message.

Just remember, you don't take cue cards to a party. Prepare but make
your presentation an informative and impactful party for all involved.
Speak from your passion and preparation to serve in the moment. Look

into their eyes, come from experience, and make sure you and your audience enjoy the ride. Keep an eye on the fuel gage and when the clock says you're nearly out of time, go back to that targeted and prepared close. Don't be a slave to a prepared speech. After all, they didn't know what you planned on saying anyway.

PLAN YOUR CLOSE FIRST

"Write the last sentence first. It is what the audience will most likely remember. Know where you're headed."

— Charles Osgood

Since the close is the last thing they will take with them from your presentation, it should come first in your preparation. When you say to a receptive audience, "So in conclusion . . . ," you have them like a fly on fly-paper. Don't let them down. Use your single 25-word sentence that summarizes the mission and purpose for your presentation as your bull's eye. It's that crisp, clear and compelling idea that makes it worth taking time for your message. Make sure your close captures your *Tah-Dah!*

If you are concerned about the length of your presentation and feel it has gone on too long, be ready with a fun way to bring them back to a summary close. "Mark Twain was at a meeting where a speaker was calling for donations. Twain was ready to donate $100. As the speaker droned on, Twain decided to cut his donation to $50. Finally, by the time the speaker finished and sent around the plate, he reached in and took a dollar out. I've learned to end before my audience does. Let me summarize my key points . . . "

Think of a current presentation you are preparing. What closing statement would help drive home and fulfill the purpose of your presentation? What would be a grab-their-minds-and-send-them-marching close? Prepare your audience's last bite from your delicious desert. Just don't let your presentation end without giving your audience a reason to remember and a reason to act in support of your mission.

POWERFUL OPENINGS

"You are an unknown quantity for only 120 seconds. After that everything you say will be heard in the context of the impression from your first two minutes."

— David Peoples

It's been said that in the first four minutes your audience will be watching and listening most intently. They are making judgments about the kind of person you are, whether they feel emotionally connected, and whether they will work with you to receive what you have to say.

If you have an introducer, give your introducer a prepared text in large print that will be no longer than a minute but long enough to establish your expertise, your topic, and the tenor of your talk.

But when it is your turn, don't leave your opening words to chance. There are a number of options that serve the same purpose – starting strong! Keep shaping and fine tuning a few standard openings on the basis of audience reactions, but always be looking for a unique opening that fits your topic, your audience, or the event.

Good openings often stimulate a need, pique curiosity and create a motivation to want to acquire what you have to say. You don't have to entertain them; show them its relevance to their career, those they serve, their life or their paycheck, and you won't bore them. What is your hook or their pain that your program is the solution to? If they have a headache, how are you the aspirin?

A good opening can honor the audience: "We are here to talk about heroes." Pause a long, long time. "They may be sitting behind you, in front of you. Or they may be you. After talking to you before the meeting, I'm impressed. You folks are the heroes. Our job is to help you stay heroes." You're honoring them in the role they play to make a difference with the information you provide.

Try starting with questions or make a statement that runs counter to expectations. Reveal a startling or unusual fact. Quote from a respected expert. "What would you do if . . . ?" "Mr. CEO recently said, . . . " Hold up a professional magazine article with a startling headline – "You may have read . . . "

Always be looking for a timely incident or amusing event that relates to the current situation, or message. Pick an anchor statement from a previous speaker or keynote. For example: "When I came to the meeting today, I overheard in the bathroom, . . . " or "Mrs. CEO started her address this morning by saying . . . "

Try an unsettling analogy: "Every morning in Africa, a gazelle wakes up. It knows it must run faster than the fastest lion or will be killed. Every morning, a lion wakes up. It knows it must outrun the slowest gazelle. It doesn't matter whether you are a lion or a gazelle, when you wake up, you are going to be running!" We're going to be running. Let me give you the information you need to keep up and run faster.

If there is time pressure, forgo the normal introduction and try a humble start: "I've always felt that introductions are a waste of time. If a speaker is any good, get on with it. If he's bad, let's get it over with. Let's get on with it. I'm here to update you on . . . "

Chip Bell talks about another advantage for memorizing your opening: "Know your first three minutes cold. Have an opening you can get through perfectly, even if you're half asleep or sick as a dog. It frees you to focus on getting your rhythm and pacing, and to build rapport with the audience instead of worrying about content." Let your opening launch you with confidence.

Whatever you do, don't fall into the all-too-common trap of using a stale joke that doesn't relate to your topic. You can overcome a bad opening, but why try when you can be prepared with a great one!

LET SEATING AND SETUP SUPPORT YOUR MISSION AND MESSAGE

"First, shape your room with the seating, and then the room will shape your speech."

— Paul Radde

Straight row setups may be easy for the hotels to figure out, but they're not conducive to energizing an audience. Try chevron or semi-circular seating that allows people to see others in the audience as they focus on you. People play off of the energy of others; let them see and hear that energy, not just your own. Don't limit your focus to the seating.

No detail is inconsequential to an effective presenter. Good speakers are as concerned about the environment they work in as they are about the group they will face. Most good speakers want to know everything about the sound system, the lighting, the staging, the screen position, and the room layout.

If story and humor are to be used in your presentation, good lighting is critical in taking advantage of expression changes. Keep good lighting on at least the portion of the platform you will be speaking from. Place the projection screen to the left or right of your presentation area. Keep it visible to you and your audience, and, if possible, dim the lights on the screen.

Joel Weldon has said, "Anything that can distract attendees will." Good speakers don't like surprises and know how effective prior planning can eliminate most of them. If your host or meeting planner doesn't show this concern, you should come early enough to take control yourself!

TAKE THE ROOM

"Get there before the audience arrives, and go up to the podium. Look out at the room. Get used to its size. Lean into the mike and speak. Say a few words; hear your voice. This will get you acclimated. It will give you a sense . . . when you take the podium, that you've been here before and nothing terrible happened."

— Peggy Noonan

You've done the basic preparation. You've worked alone or with the support staff to know your equipment, check lighting, and find out where your backup microphone will be if needed. But now it's time to *take the room.* That's right! Go to where you will be speaking and positively visualize the presentation performance you are about to give.

Create reminder cues. From memory or from notes, review your key points and tie each key point or story to a different object in your field of view from the platform. Whenever you get lost in your thoughts, look at the appropriate object and the key content will be triggered when you need it most.

Finally, get ready to enjoy another presentation. Think of programs you have done in similar rooms and the energy people give to you and the meeting. Count yourself blessed, thankful again for the opportunity to present a message that makes a difference.

MAKE SURE YOU SPEAK TO "FRIENDS"

"Arrive early to meet and greet the audience members. It builds rapport and creates an environment where they're no longer strangers."

— Chip Bell

As people begin to arrive before your presentation begins, introduce yourself to as many audience members as possible. Greet them, introduce yourself with a smile, and extend a handshake as you ask for their name.

Try some winning questions designed to get even the most difficult to warm up: What are the biggest challenges these people are facing? What works for you in handling those challenges? From what you see, what do the people in this organization really need to hear? What speaker have you liked the best and why?

Early in your speech, share some of their best input and make the audience members look good by giving them the credit by name. Then watch for the nods and the looks that will say, "Hey, this speaker is good. He knows who to listen to around here!"

Don't be afraid to approach the most threatening members you see. Early conversations can change potential critics into fan club members before you even take the platform. As Ben Franklin used to say, "The best way to win someone over to your cause is ask them to help you."

In short, why speak to strangers or enemies when with a little work you can convert them into a receptive fan. It's easier to speak to people who have already decided to like you.

TURN ANXIETY
INTO POSITIVE TENSION

"After 30 years of the Tonight Show, Johnny Carson's heart rate went from 64 bpm up to 134 bpm just before going on stage. He let his extra energy add to his magnetism. Expect your humor to work instead of fearing it will bomb. Positive focus easily turns anxiety into excitement."

— Carla Rieger

Even the best speakers don't eliminate nervousness; they control and use it. But the more you try to control stage fright, the easier it is for it to control you as a speaker. Edward Newman, the newscaster, put it well: "The goal is never to get rid of your butterflies but to have your butterflies fly in formation."

Try a change in perspective and actions. See "anxiety" as "excitement" and then use it to energize your presentation. If you weren't excited at all, you wouldn't be motivated to prepare to do a quality presentation. Remember, tension can be transformed into fuel for purposeful movement at the front of a room or on the platform. Instead of locking your knees and gripping a lectern, risk moving. Excited presenters move to transform excitement into purposeful impact.

If you often forget key points, try establishing memory cues to help you retain presentation material. Go into the program room before the program. Anchor key program points to specific items in the room: the clock, a picture, each door, or picture. In your mind's eye, put each point on a different item in sequence. While speaking walk your eyes in sequence around the room as you go through your speech. When you feel a blank, look at the next item and your point will come back to you. Memory triggers will help you find all of your key points.

Learn to breathe to relax before and during your talk. Before you go on, take five to 10 deep breaths. A deep breath gets your heart rate down and oxygenates your blood. Using a healthy pause with a deep breath can get you centered again during your talk.

Don't be afraid when you go blank. Take action:

• Take a moment to move; look up and away to collect your thoughts.

• Laugh at yourself and ask for help, "I have lost my train of thought. It will come back, but until then I have been blessed with an entirely new direction." They will laugh; they have all been there.

• Have the group review your past key points; your next point will often return during the review. Ask, "This is a good time for review to see if you were listening. What was my last point and where was I going?"

• Go to your note card and take time to find your next phrase that will unlock the next point (Your cards should contain single words or phrases that can remind you of the key points . . . not the exact script).

Some speakers show their anxiety and inexperience by the overuse of such "verbal crutches" or fillers – their use of filler language - their "likes," "umms," "ya knows," or "I means." A certain number of fillers are normal, but when speakers flip into overuse, they can come across as unfocused and unprepared. Once aware of the problem, learn to replace "umms" with short reflective pauses. People have more of a tolerance for snippets of silence than a stream of filler phrases. It sometimes helps to slow down the rate of your speaking. You don't have to race; a varied pace increases attention.

If you continue having anxiety problems, try joining a local Toastmasters group for you to practice speaking. Many designate an "Umm Counter" to help you catch yourself and to find alternatives. In the face of continued anxiety, learn to speak more!

Finally, don't be afraid to laugh at yourself and share your anxiety. Try saying, "Some speakers get butterflies. I think today, I have eagles. Bear with me here as I get them to soar in formation." When people laugh with you, the comfort generated is often all you will need to capture the power in the enlivening tension and excitement that you feel.

AUDIENCES WANT TO LOVE YOU

"The majority of audiences are composed of a few hundred mildly pleased, mildly bored people who in most cases have to be there. This should not be disheartening but inspiring. You, the speaker, get to wake them up, get to get them thinking about things they might not otherwise have thought about. They appreciate . . . humor as an unexpected gift. They are polite to boring speakers, but when someone shows up with good material, they're actually moved."

— Peggy Noonan

Instead of being intimidated by that next audience, see them as a pocket of boredom in search of a happening! They are often expecting the worst – another boring meeting. If you give them meaningful information and give them a bit of fun and inspiration while presenting, they'll love you.

Keep in mind, most audiences want you to be successful to prove to them and others that it was worth taking the time to attend. Remember, the greatest gift you can give any team is to cancel a meeting; it's *free time!* You get to prove them wrong.

Their mothers taught them to sit there politely and stare; you get to show them that they can actually enjoy good, productive meetings. Don't worry. If you're boring, they will forget you. If you inspire and inform, they just may remember you long enough to tell someone else about you so you can do this all over again. For professional speakers that's the name of the game – being remembered long enough to be referred and rehired!

YOU WON'T WIN THEM ALL

"Loosen up; you're not going to convince 'em anyway. Speeches aren't about turning archenemies into cheering supporters. Presentations are mainly opportunities to reassure those who already agree with you that you're a horse worth betting on."

— Tom Peters

Let's be realistic. Most audiences want fresh windows that add a little depth, a few new facts and interesting tangents that can enliven what they already know. I used to feel upset when I would read an evaluation that said, "Some of this I have heard before." I no longer feel that way.

I realized that if everything participants learned in my programs was new, they would be in deep trouble anyway. I'm not here to blaze entirely new trails but to provide a window with a view that lets them experience an often common truth in a new, fresh way.

Having to impress them all can also get in the way. I once was told by a frustrated meeting planner, "I'm disappointed. You're so good, and you're not doing it today. Ninety-five percent of the people in this room are loving what you are saying, but you spent two-thirds of your time trying to convince the other 5% of your audience to like you. For your information, those are the same people that have never liked any speaker we have brought in here."

I had given control of my presentation to the few at the expense of the many. Learn to focus on serving up your best for those who are there to participate and learn, and never expect to impress them all. Even Jesus reportedly knew the limits of a great sermon. After speaking in parables, he frequently said, "He who has ears, let him hear." That's not a bad perspective for you to keep when speaking to what seems like a tough audience.

SMILE AND LOOK LIKE YOU ENJOY IT

"Never act as if the job were a chore. Act as if you regarded this as a great opportunity to say something that needs saying or that you have wanted to tell somebody for a long time."

— Charles Osgood

Don't give them excuses; give them a performance. Don't just tell them you are honored to be there; show them they count. Don't complain about the lack of numbers; speak about the quality of those that showed up. Instead of matching your face to the Stoic in the front row, when you walk on stage, take a deep breath and put a smile on your face.

All the statistics in the world can't measure the impact of a good smile. A smile is catchy; once you give it away to your audience, you'll find it's easy to get it back from them. Don't stop with a smile. Let your face and your body visually stimulate the eyes of your audience with the same message your words are trying to communicate to their ears.

In one sentence – Get your face and body "out of park." Be easy to watch as people listen. Unless you have authority or until you are famous, you must sell people on listening by conveying in a persuasive manner what you have to say. In fact, even if you are famous, you won't stay that way long unless you learn to honor the privilege of the platform. To the best, this is not a job; it is a calling. When called, perform.

USE SUCCESSFUL SPEAKERS
AS ANCHORS

"If you are speaking at 4 pm, get to the meeting at 7:30 am. Listen to every other speaker that goes on before you. Then when you speak, help tie the entire day together by linking the previous presentations to yours."

— Joe Calloway, CSP, CPAE

Following a great speaker ought to be easier; the audience is already warmed up and ready to respond. Consciously try to borrow on the enthusiasm for other speakers who have preceded you by *anchoring* their success into your program.

Instead of being intimidated by what they did, use the enthusiasm and the insights they have already generated. By acknowledging another's effectiveness and message you honor the audience for liking a good speaker. You also signal that they can expect more of the same from your part of the meeting.

If the speaker is in your audience, acknowledge their success early in your program – "Those of you who were in Mary's audience had the opportunity to see a master at work. She's here with us. Let's give her a round of applause." Be ready to reference key quotes they used that help transition to your presentation's focus. Don't compete against other speakers; bring them onto your team so you can both make a difference.

TALK TO INDIVIDUALS
ONE AT A TIME

"Never talk to a group. Talk to just one listener at a time. Look directly at him for five seconds . . . and then look at somebody else. It gives the speaker a sense of talking private-ly."

— Charlie Windhorst

Speaking can be as simple as having a *conversation* with your audience one set of eyeballs at a time. Talking to individuals builds engagement and rapport. If you're nervous, start by picking three friendly faces that seem alert, alive, and responsive to what's going on. Pick one to the left, one in the center, then one to the right. By talking to all three you hit the whole audience.

When you conclude a sentence or make a point, learn to be comfortable with looking at a face in your audience for a second or two before concluding the sentence. This is called "landing your message."

Slow, decisive eye contact communicates confidence. People will pay more attention to you, and it slows your speaking pace. Look at each person for five seconds and then move to the next person. It gives a sense of talking privately. With practice, you'll learn to enjoy every person your eyes meet, and they will enjoy you.

MAKE PEOPLE FEEL IMPORTANT

"As speakers, we aren't the wings. We are the wind beneath the wings."

— Roxanne Emmerich, CSP

Mary Kay Ash, the founder of Mary Kay Cosmetics always tells her sales associates to pretend that everyone they meet has a sign on their chest that reads, "Make Me Feel Important." The same can be said for every speaker that addresses an audience.

Treat every audience member as a VIP. A VIP deserves the best you have to offer. It will show in your eye contact, your smile, your listening ear, and your thoughtful reply to every question. If you're really into customer service, that makes speakers servants. Let it show in all you do, and audiences will respond.

Take time to make as many in your audience part of your team as you can. Tim Richardson, CSP, suggests, ""I sometimes meet people in my audience who look really good-natured and will ask them if I can tell one of my stories to them, and then I do!" Not only will it make them feel special, it will energize your performance as you feed off of their enthusiastic support they are all too ready to provide. .

ADMIT MISTAKES EARLY

"When I transformed my hidden insecurities to radiant self-doubt, I learned the secret of true charisma on the platform. Give up trying to exude confidence. Rather, practice projecting 'vibrant vulnerability.'"

— Lee Glickstein

When Martin Luther was quoted as saying, "Sin boldly," I'm sure he was not trying out new slogans for loose living. Luther knew that to live was to risk inevitable mistakes, but that we were called to live full, vibrant lives anyway.

The truly confident in any age don't dread or hide their errors, they seem to celebrate them as proof they are seizing life's challenges. In fact, never be afraid of putting egg on your face early in a presentation. As we have said, the only perfect public speakers are in training films. Don't hesitate to laugh at yourself when you make those mistakes. It helps humanize you and your presentation.

People often come to presentations to know that they are not alone. My admitting mistakes and learning from them, you connect with an audience full of people who are fully aware of their own mistakes and want to improve. You let them know you can.

After all, you don't want them leaving a training experience impressed with you and feeling inadequate themselves. Your job is not creating standing ovations, but influencing lasting changes that make a difference for those attending.

By letting them know you're not perfect, you also throw off those in the audience who want desperately to prove that you are not. By admitting it early, their game is over.

PROMOTE LASTING CHANGE

"To impress is an ego game; to influence is a behavior game! Do you make evaluations and standing ovations or do you make a difference?"

— Mark Sanborn, CSP, CPAE

A good speaker wants lasting impact from a presentation, not just a standing ovation. To improve your impact, have participants take *Keeper Notes*, limiting their notes to one page of key ideas, phrases or quotes that will remind them of what they want to take away from the presentation. Challenge them to take time at the end of the presentation to focus their change efforts on three targeted "Keepers" worth developing. Focus on those that they are motivated to do and that have a strategic value to their organization.

If time permits, have participants share their goals with others as a way of summarizing the program. Suggest ways they can keep the ball rolling for self-change: Place Post-its® with their key goals on their daily calendar and read it daily; create their own reminder recording of key quotes to add to their digital play list; and use self-reward to make change worthwhile. Don't let participants get away with enthusiastic evaluations when you're called to help them focus their development on strategic change. No one needs another speech; they want wisdom and practical strategies that produce lasting results.

You may also want to encourage participants to start their own "Keeper Log" folder. Many top leaders journal their key ideas, activities and valued quotes to keep their history and to serve them in the future. Instead of using a traditional journal, try encouraging participants to send themselves an email at the end of the day. Include: something they did to move forward their development goals, quotes that impacted them, and personal stories/examples of best practice in action. The next morning, suggest they review the previous day's email to start that day's positive momentum. After reading, have them move the email to their "Keeper Log" folder. These saved messages are now searchable and can prove invaluable in finding the quotes, stories, and personal examples that can enliven their future presentations and document their development progress at their next personnel evaluation.

THERE IS POWER IN PACING

"Pace, pace, pace. Vary your style. Animation in facial variety and movement. I don't plan either. It comes because I believe in the material."

— Eileen McDargh, CSP, CPAE

Don't wear your audience out with any one style or activity. Be able to talk fast and slow. Weave your message from heart, to head, to humor. Physically move toward the audience and then away. Remember the difference between *Raiders of the Lost Ark* and *The Temple of Doom*. The first film paced the viewer from action, to comedy, to romance, and then back again. The second film was a never-ending, audience-dulling stream of action. One set records; the second did not.

Vary the tempo by speeding up and slowing down. Get louder and then softer. Learn to vary your rate, tone, pitch, content, and activity level. By doing so, you, like the masters in the speaking world, can create a kind of centrifugal force that pulls listeners into your message and your mission.

Just when the audience feels they can take no more, provide a respite, slowing to allow moments of rest before again surging to new heights with a new example or stirring quote. Working at pacing translates into powerful presenting to your audiences.

KEEP IT SIMPLE

"Among my earliest recollections, I remember how, when a mere child, I used to get irritated when anybody talked to me in a way I could not understand. After hearing the neighbors talk with my father, I would spend the night walking up and down, trying to make out what was the exact meaning of some of their, to me, dark sayings. I could not sleep when I got on such a hunt after an idea, until I had caught it; and I was not satisfied until I had put it in language plain enough, as I thought, for any boy I knew to comprehend. This was a kind of passion with me, and it has stuck by me."

— Abraham Lincoln

We should expect nothing less from today's speakers. Lincoln was one of our country's best Presidents and most effective orators. He knew the importance of good stories and simple language in connecting to his audiences. He knew, first and foremost, that speakers had to touch people and that even the most important message must first be simple enough to understand.

The Gettysburg Address had a beautiful simplicity and compelling force that in just minutes was able to capture the hearts and minds of a whole country for the ages. Complexity and strength are no match for simple truths said with focus and commitment. What are you doing to keep your message and stories poignant and easy to understand?

USE PARTICIPATION POWER
TO ENLIVEN YOUR PRESENTATION

"Today's audiences are considerably different. They are not content to be 'talked at,' but rather want to be a part of the program. Learning need not be a spectator sport! If your presentation on training style involves your attendees, you'll quickly sense a more attentive and interested audience."
— Edward E. Scannell, CSP

Participation is like a wild card in poker. When the wild card is played, it almost always results in a winning hand.

Thankfully, there are many creative ways to get audiences constructively involved in your presentation. A good presenter knows how to use participation. By involving your audience, you get an opportunity to honor their input, their concerns and their value. By mastering innovative strategies you can communicate your confidence in the material you are presenting – you are so confident that you are not afraid of opening yourself to the input of others.

Participation can help you reengage your audience, surface the wisdom and experience of your audience and surface relevant questions and concerns. Here are some tips worth using:

1. Short dyad exercises can be useful for presenters. Don't be afraid to use it early with tough audiences. Sometimes quiet audiences are not unhappy with the speaker; they may very well be uncomfortable with the strangers sitting around them. An early exercise lets them connect to a neighbor and ease anxiety.

2. Use something that involves simple on-target questions and non-threatening disclosure. Prepare questions and activities to reinforce every major point in your speech.

3. To ensure retention and processing, stop and ask participants to paraphrase the keepers they have picked up from the talk. Ask for

any questions of clarification. By doing this frequently you send a message to the people that you expect them to listen and process what they are hearing.

4. Tell people in your audience that you want them to share their successes and what they learned that has worked. Don't be afraid to share the ideas generated by your audience. Sometimes the most knowledgeable person in the room is sitting in the audience. Be ready to make them part of your team and give them the credit for their valuable input. There is an added benefit – Audience best practice stories are rich with value for future programs as stories you can retell.

5. Try using the "callout technique" – have each person listening write down two ideas or questions and then call on a specific person you know is participating to share one item. You've given them time to prepare and it communicates that anyone could be called on to be involved.

6. People like quizzes; insert a three question quiz on a slide. If they get the answers right, you can skip most of the content on the next series of slides.

7. To keep attention and keep your audience involved, move and ask open-ended questions to people near you.

Remember, getting audiences to participate in an active way pays off in enthusiasm, commitment to change, and learning that sticks. Honoring your audience is one of the best ways to ensure that they will return the favor by honoring you.

NEW vs. USED PARTNERS

"I always 'buddy-up' participants with someone they don't know, or know the least. You can hide out mentally by yourself, but when you are required to participate with a new acquaintance, you need to 'show up' physically and mentally. When the buddies get to know each other and share a secret, they now have a bond because we have a special part no one else knows."

— Brian Lee, CSP

Getting audiences to participate in an active way pays off in generating enthusiastic audiences. Even in very large audiences short participation exercises can be used to get people out of their comfort zone and into your message.

But when encouraging small group exercises have them pick a "new" vs. a "used" partner. Try saying: "Find a partner here that you do not know. I consider people you know or work with frequently as 'used people.' You can't pick a 'used person.' Those of you that are assertive get to pick your partner; those that are not I will pair up."

People don't participate well with "used" people; they almost always follow directions with partners they don't know. Participating with a stranger builds a bridge to a new person; it also focuses and energizes the exercise. A presenter's job is not just to inform; it is also to encourage constructive networking across and within the organization.

INCORPORATE THEIR STORY

"The most important trait of a presenter is that sense of humility that says, 'I'm here as a fellow traveler and we are going to learn together.' Good presentations are a partnership, not a monologue."

— Chip Bell

A speech that is limited to a monologue fails to take advantage of the wisdom of those attending. Our job as presenters is to facilitate the transfer of wisdom wherever it originates. The biggest difference between being enthusiastic and generating enthusiasm is whose ideas you get excited about.

Whatever happens in your audience, be ready to use it. Don't just bring enthusiasm and energy to the podium; feed off the enthusiasm of your audience wherever you find it. Don't just look for it; acknowledge it. Whenever I end an animated dyad exercise, I ask how they enjoyed it. When they nod with approval, I add, "That's why I had to stop you! You're enjoying this too much."

Your eyes can listen to and touch your audience. Let them see the spark in your eyes and pause long enough to see the spark in theirs. With practice, your eye contact can grab every person in that room. Once you have them, don't let them go until you draw out an ounce of energy in return.

Remember, don't be afraid to share the ideas generated by your audience. Sometimes the most knowledgeable person in the room is sitting in your meeting. Be ready to make them part of your team and give them the credit for their valuable input.

STORY TELLING FACTS
WORTH SHARING

"When telling a story, don't fill in what will help them relate."

— Barry Mann

By sharing detailed descriptions in your stories, you waste precious time and make it harder for the audience to connect and build their own experience. Let them fill most of the facts for themselves.

After all, even though my dog is a Dalmatian, I don't have to tell them that to complete my story. The dog in their story will be more enjoyable to them if you allow it to be their favorite breed instead of yours. After all the dog does not need to be told that she is a Dalmatian.

If the audience doesn't need to know, go for brevity over completeness. Each member of your audience will enjoy painting his own pictures in his mind's eye. Let your story become their story by allowing them to fill in the blanks with their dog, their airport, their partner, their office, . . . their life.

In the world of business, long stories can waste time better spent on practical content. By keeping stories short without unnecessary detail and focused on the mission message, your stories will be appreciated, remembered and repeated.

DEVELOP A TIGHT
BUT POWERFUL DELIVERY

"The sound bite is the ultimate in making every word tell. It is the very soul of compactness. Brevity is not enough. You need weight. Hence some sound bites qualify for greatness: F.D.R's 'The only thing to fear is fear itself' or Reagan's 'Tear down the wall.'"

— Charles Krauthhammer

Brevity is critical to a good speaker or leader. The average length of a humor bit in a speech is 15 seconds, and nothing will kill a story like unnecessary length. Humor writer Larry Wilde says it like few can, "If you can't hit oil in 20 seconds, stop boring." When it's short, even if people don't laugh at your humor, at least they haven't wasted too much of their time.

With a humorous story, maintain tension by building your story quickly toward resolution. Never slow it down by giving unnecessary information or taking tangents. Twist your lines, juggle words around and chop until you have a tight, but funny story that works. Don't just keep it short; speak at a brisk pace and accelerate into the clear punch line.

Don't limit your brevity to your humor; learn to drop unnecessary words and craft the flow for all of your stories and key statements. If you want to be quoted, don't settle for an insight. Work that insight to be tight, impactful, and memorable. Often, your audiences will help you. Listen to their takeaway lines or "Keepers." They will give you a hint of what is impactful and easy to remember. Once you have isolated that powerful quote, use it often as an "anchor line" for your talks.

MASTER THE PAUSE

"Be courageous enough to pause and give your audience time to think. That means slowing down your points of wisdom so there is time for the 'penny to drop.'"

— Ron Arden

Whether sharing practical insights, a moving or informative story, or a funny incident, master the use of the pause. Time your pauses to give your audience time to visualize the story and grasp the situation you are creating so that when you give the punch line or twist the story, the impact will be even more effective.

If you are using a pause with humor, you may raise your eyebrows, look to the side and smile, or look at one of your best laughers. The pause allows the audience to catch up, connect the story to their lives, and begin to guess their own punch line. After all, part of the fun of humor for any audience is trying to guess where the story is headed. Then when you add your own special twist, that train wreck of the brain that happens when you deliver a great punch line, a hearty laugh is the payoff for all involved.

Finally, as comedians will tell you, "Don't step on your own lines." When you finish a story, stop, smile and wait for their response. Too many novices don't pause long enough and move on before the audience has a chance to absorb, appreciate and react.

As a leader presenting, pause, pause, . . . pause! Pause just before you state a key point, just after you state a key point, and just before moving on to the next segment of your presentation. Let your message sink in.

Mark Twain once said, "The right word may be effective, but no word was ever as effective as a rightly timed pause." Study the leaders, presenters and professional speakers you most respect to understand the impact of a positive pause. Start experimenting with what you learn.

HAVE FUN PRESENTING

"I don't tell funny stories; I tell stories funny."

— Jerry Clower

Forget all that serious training you had as a child. Show that you enjoy spreading meaningful messages and good cheer. Keep your eyes on your listener's eyes to capture their attention and build your confidence.

You may want to embrace a new word, "Neoteny," which means "maturing but retaining childlike qualities." Good humorists and professional speakers let their "child" show for fun and profit. When you use humor, give yourself permission to be a bit of a "ham" and show your enjoyment and emotions. Exaggeration is a big part of humor and good storytelling; let your face and gestures help paint the picture.

Does your voice have life? Does it elevate a bit when you ask a question? Does it dance as your heart warms to a particular story? Does it convey your enthusiasm? Play with your expressiveness when you are presenting.

If you've got an exciting message, you shouldn't be able to hide it. Animation has impact. Once you have start presenting, make eye contact with at least two people, then, to the extent that business attire allows, risk floating like a butterfly, stinging like a bee. That may be a bit extreme for you, but you can still tell your story with energy, make the point, and call them to action.

Be enthusiastic even if you have to act a bit. They buy your content when you do. Never act as if your job were a chore. Act as if you regarded this as a great opportunity to say something that needed to be said or that you have wanted to tell them for a long time. Make that audience and your message feel important! Of course, as a leader, it's important to have serious moments, but don't ever major in seriousness if you want to have an impact . . . and want to be invited back.

USE ANCHOR LINES

"To anchor your key ideas in participants' minds, connect a major principle with a story that includes a movement, gesture, or catchy statement they can repeat later to each other as a means of re-enforcing the concept."

— Lou Heckler, CSP, CPAE

The name of the game is not just entertaining an audience; you want to have what you say be retained. That is why advertisers use catchy messages that they repeat in ad after ad. They not only use their words to impact viewers; They tie the phrases to characters and images that once established act as reminders of the product or service whenever they are seen or heard.

As a presenter, you can benefit from the same principles. Work hard on your delivery of key punch lines by making the key phrase memorable and your delivery unique in pace, gestures and look.

Once established take your audience back to that story whenever it applies by using the same phrase and delivery. They will laugh again and again each time the point is reinforced. With any luck your catch phrase may become a permanent part of that company or association's vocabulary. To borrow a successful catch phrase, "Just do it!"

USE POWERPOINT TO SUPPORT
NOT CONTROL YOUR PRESENTATION

"Business people are always describing the future with bullet points. That's stupifying. If you put people to sleep; they don't remember a thing."

— Noel Tichy

PowerPoint without context doesn't work. There is no one answer to how to construct the deck for your program. It's how well you use the ones you create. Think of your slides as spices in a recipe, and too many spices can spoil the recipe. They didn't come to see slides; they want your point of view and to be impacted by your presentation and the information you are sharing. Visual aids are to enhance and support. That is why they came after you have constructed your message.

First, decide what you want to say. What are your points of wisdom? How can you illustrate these points best? Use your support material to support your case, not be your case. Don't just create 40 *PowerPoint* slides and then decide what to say between them. Get your purpose and vital messages clear first.

When you have the choice, include the key prompts in a series of simple *PowerPoint* slides. Design points that are not complete sentences but that launch your content to be shared. Use a standard style and font-size that your audience can get used to reading. Here are seven tips to consider:

1. Think one hour of preparation per slide. The better you get, the less time it will take. Too many practice the content of the slide while not taking time to think through the stories, transitions, stories, elaboration or analogies that can be used to bring it that slide to life. Once you have isolated this additional content, work at weaving them together for your talk. Have content that allows you to take more or less time as the situation requires.

2. No matter what slides you have, never be trapped by an over-filled *PowerPoint* program. Now, if the exact wording you use for legal purposes is more important than how you say it, be prepared to include and read that part of your message.

3. Talk to people, not the slides. If you read a quote to time the response to its message, use the front monitor instead of turning your back to the audience. Glance at what is on the screen or the monitor in front of you and then take your attention back to the audience.

4. If you have many insights on a slide but want to focus on just a few key points, show the slide and pause to let the audience absorb the contents of the slide while you look at your notes in silence. Don't let it be too long, but move towards one of the people in the audience and begin speaking to them in support of the key information you want them to remember.

5. Instead of using a build with numerous bullet points, some information is better conveyed in a more memorable graph or table. Experiment with different capabilities to enliven your content. If you are using a quote from someone you have interviewed, ask if they are comfortable with you taking a picture and doing a quick digital recording of them reading their own quote. With their permission, you can place both in a slide so they can see the person and hear the quote from the source.

6. At strategic points, provide an interesting slide – "Wrong Way – Do Not Enter!" then tell them why there are some counter-indications that they should be aware of! When sending a message that is important, use some form of the words *"important"* and *"different"* to unlock the listening potential of your audience. Encourage others to provide verbal preambles to heighten your attention: "Here's something *important* I need you to consider . . . " "There's something *different* you need to be aware of . . . " Instead of promoting scanning, such phrases demand effective listening from even busy people.

7. Use an advancer that is wireless and allows you to advance slides and use a pointer from anywhere in your room. No one likes being strapped to a computer. If your advancer allows, turn off the screen when you want the focus to return to you as a speaker.

If you want more information, try accessing
www.presentation-pointers.com or
www.presentations.com to find tips.

MAKE YOUR Q&A WORK

"The most important trait of a presenter is that sense of humility that says, 'I'm here as a fellow traveler and we are going to learn together.' Good presentations are a partnership, not a monologue."

— Chip Bell

Nothing can make or break the impact of your message more than how you handle Q&A. Keep in mind that your goal is to reinforce the purpose of the meeting, establish a strong audience connection, clarify key points and ensure relevance and understanding.

Q&A can be a very enlivening and informative part of your presentation. Hope for tough questions and view your audience as a resource and a teacher. They often know the answers that you don't. If you don't know the answer, admit it. Share about how frequently the answer is often found in your impressive audiences. If not, you can get back to them using your company resources to supply needed information. Here are seven tips for handling Q&A.

1. If you sense people might have questions, don't ignore it or put the person on the spot. Say, "What I just said often gives rise to some questions. Does anyone have a question?" Make the second person looked at be the person you sensed had a question. By doing so, you make it safe to ask questions or disagree.

2. When a question is asked, make sure to repeat the question so that the entire audience can hear. That gives you an extra moment to prepare your response. When you answer, answer to the entire audience, not just the person asking the question. Always weave your answer back to the central theme of your talk. Don't allow questions to take you away from the reason you are there.

3. If prior to a program, you find a participant asks an important question, say, "Rather than answer that now, I'd like to use that as the first question during Q&A. Getting that first question is always tough; yours is perfect. Would you mind asking it then?"

4. With a tough question, look at the person directly while they ask the question, and then look to others as you answer it. If you keep looking at the difficult questioner, he's all too likely to interrupt your response as though you were the only two people in the room.

5. Assume any question has merit until proven otherwise. If you don't see how something connects to your topic, probe: "I'm not sure I follow/understand. Help me understand." If the question is complex, reply to the part that relates to most of the audience and promise to discuss other aspects after the program or during the break.

6. If you don't understand their question even after probing, try humor: "I'm sorry. I think I missed my coffee fix this morning. Somebody is going to have to say it much slower and louder for me. And please dumb it down a couple of grade levels for me." That puts the problem on you, not them. If it continues, take part of what you understood and reframe a response around that and promise to talk later after the program or during a break.

7. With a loaded question, repeating it for those who have not heard allows you to restate the question in a less loaded rephrasing. Always try to conclude your answer by referencing the central theme of the meeting focus. Sometimes you can say, "I know that is a question you are passionate about. I'd like you to write that out; let's look at that during the break or later during Q&A as time permits."

Don't stop learning in these important areas. Take time to observe and learn from others you respect. What have you seen others do that could help you make Q&A work in your presentation?

ENLIVEN YOUR VIDEOCONFERENCING AND TELECONFERENCING PRESENTATIONS

With increasing frequency, we are asked to present to teams where the members are from different geographic locations. While we would like to always be able to meet in person, that is often not possible. Many organizations are using teleconferencing and videoconferencing to convey information and stay connected. When leaders use these technologies to present, they need to make the most of their electronic connection. The basic rules on power communication continue to apply, but here are some tips to help make teleconferencing and videoconferencing go smoothly.

1. Know your system. Surprisingly some 75 percent of video conferences don't work the first time due to a lack of understanding of the technology. Take time to learn how to use the technology or contact your video conferencing provider to ensure they can easily facilitate your video conference. Unless you have dropped $50,000 to $150,000 on your video conferencing setup, you won't have perfectly smooth, indistinguishable-from-real-life video. So, you need to work within the limitations of you and your participant's equipment and bandwidth. The most important thing to remember is to keep your gestures small and your movements slower than normal. A little attention to this detail will minimize any choppy effects.

2. With large conferences, assign a chairperson/moderator. Running a video conference, which can include three to 30 sites with potentially thousands of participants, is no easy feat. Be sure your chairperson is an effective manager who can command the attention of a large number of people.

3. Appoint someone other than moderator to take meeting minutes. This increases the perceived value of the meeting. Whoever is taking

minutes should also have their phone muted because the clicking of typing will be too distracting for others.

4. Do your pre and post work. Provide an agenda and specific start and stop times before the meeting. Recap items at close of meeting and email summary within 24 hours.

5. Keep visuals simple and supportive of your objectives and message. Use the horizontal (landscape) format. Share content appropriately – Studies show video conference participants respond favorably at a ratio of people 80% of the time and content 20%.

6. Dress professionally for videoconferencing. Your cloths say a lot about you, but through a video conference, some clothes say it loudly. To provide the best view of you, try to dress in light pastels and muted colors. Bright, loud colors can make your skin look weird on screen. Don't wear all-light or all-dark colors to avoid any white balance or contrast issues. Busy patterns too are something to avoid.

7. Stay in one place. Check your visibility on screen to be sure you have not moved out of range of sight during the conference. Also, avoid fidgeting. Rustling papers or tapping pens can be distracting to other participants.

8. Use a headset with a microphone in front. It allows your hands to be free to manage the equipment and make more natural gestures. Speak naturally and clearly with a normal volume and tone. There is no need to raise your voice or yell into the microphone.

9. The best place to look while speaking is directly into the camera lens. Your participants will get the impression that you are looking directly at them. This creates a more trustworthy, congenial experience between them and you. Try to be as "natural" and relaxed as you can. Use natural gestures when you speak. Use the preview mode to best adjust your camera angle and try to fill the screen as much as possible with people – rather than with other distracting room details.

10. If time permits, introduce everyone on the conference. Give people a chance to acknowledge that they are connected and can hear you, the leader. Not only will this help break the ice, but will also allow you to hear their volume and sound quality.

11. Pause briefly for others to answer your questions or to make comments. Since the audio has a very slight delay and it can be difficult to join the conversation when you can't make eye contact, use more pauses.

12. Encourage give and take — questions and answers. They are the bedrock of communication. In a video conference, you are hampered by not having everyone in front of you. This is especially apparent when you ask a question, as it is sometimes difficult for your participants to know who you are talking to. Make sure you say a person's name at the beginning of your question. When you ask someone a question, make sure you give them a few seconds to respond. This allows them time to unmute themselves. In seeking consensus, couch your questions to address the least amount of responses. For example, don't ask if everyone understands; ask who doesn't understand or agree.

AVOID GIVING THE WHOLE LOAD

"The secret of being a bore is to tell everything."

— Voltaire

Just because you have prepared to say it, doesn't mean you have to share it. A good speaker doesn't dump data. They deliver a targeted, meaningful message that influences those who hear it.

We are already in information overload; some have described it as if we are sipping through a straw at a fire hydrant. Don't add to it. People want you to be a broker for relevant wisdom they can use. People are on a treasure hunt, and you take them to the treasure. After all, just because you have a library card, doesn't mean you have to read every book. Just because you have done the research, doesn't mean you have to prove it by listing all of your findings on a crowded PowerPoint deck.

Be true to your research by developing your core points and a variety of ways to make those points. Then be a steward of their time by sharing only what you feel will maximize the effectiveness of your message. To help you avoid the last minute rapid-mouth overload, plan alternate close points in your presentation that allow you to transition to the story and points you want to close with that still accomplish your mission.

AVOID THE BLAME FRAME

"Never complain about anything in front of the audience: it makes you look bad."

— Patricia Fripp, CSP, CPAE

When in pain, we want to find someone to blame. Some speakers rail at the audio people; others glare at the meeting planner or logistics team. Still others pout before the audience in a personalized version of "Poor me!"

Avoid the blame frame! Use your positive energy to pull your audience to you as your support team works to correct the problem. The audio team already feels bad enough about any problem; don't add to it. You want them putting their energy into fixing the problem, not getting even with you for making them look bad.

The best leaders and presenters take more than their share of the blame and less than their share of the credit. After the presentation, you'll get more credit and compliments for your professionalism, and others will apologize profusely for the problem even occurring.

Learn this important lesson early — never blame people from the platform. If you must, confront the problem privately later. Keep in mind, everyone makes mistakes and some staging problems are no one's fault! Don't get even; work to get results by working as a team!

MICROPHONE COVERUPS
WORTH KNOWING

"Things turn out the best for those who make the best of the way things turn out."

— John Wooden

There are no dress rehearsals, and the only place that perfect presenters exist are in educational movies. When the microphone pops, whines, or just plain dies, be ready with humorous comeback that can turn your disaster into a memorable performance.

The movies work because they have a ready script. Do you have lines you are ready to use that you know will work? Create your own microphone cover lines for your next disaster or master some of mine:

"How many of you in the back of the room read lips?"

"Obviously, someone in the control room has already heard me before."

"All right God, I'll change the subject!"

"Whatever that noise is, it's getting closer!"

"You know, I'm actually starting to like that squeal."

"Is this microphone mating season or something?"

Whatever you do, don't fight it or panic; use it. After all; soon your current microphone disaster may be a very good story.

SCRIPTED COVERUPS
FOR EVERY OCCASION

"The game of life is not so much holding a good hand as play-ing a poor hand well."

— H. T. Leslie

Don't limit your preparation to microphone problems. The hallmark of a great speaker is how well they recover from whatever happens. Instead of worrying about doing a perfect presentation, be concerned about bouncing back quickly to serve.

The biggest headaches in order of frustration to speakers are: Projector failure, computer freeze, software glitch, connection problems, and dead batteries/power problems. Be ready for the common headaches and men-tally visualize a problem and how you would handle it.

Disasters prey only on perfectionists. Things go wrong for all humans! Why not you? Sudden emergencies can and will happen. Embrace the un-known and emergencies as eventually endearing stories. Even the worst disasters are great learning experiences. Learn to love the craziness of life; no writer could make some of this stuff up.

Work to develop "Prepared Spontaneity." Being able to laugh at yourself helps you let go and bounce back to attack the problem anew. Even disas-ters can build increased enthusiasm when you control your response by using *prepared "Savers"* designed for the times unexpected challenges occur. Here's a collection of *"Savers"* you can memorize and use to take the terror out of speaker disasters:

- "This is the part of the program where we . . . (whatever hap-pens). From now on, the program will take an upswing!"

- "The ability to be cool under fire is such a great skill. I wish I had it."

- "Just my luck — the light at the end of the tunnel is a locomotive."

- "Have any of you seen my mother; she usually handles things like this for me."

• (When only one laughs) "If you could just run around the room while you are laughing, it would sound like everyone enjoyed that one."

• (When they fail to respond to questions) A)" When you guys get quiet, you don't mess around. You're professionals." B) "That was a good question/joke in rehearsal; even the mirror responded/laughed."

• (When under time pressure) "With the time challenges we're facing, I've decided to take out everything that is unessential from my talk. (Pause) So in conclusion . . . " Once they laugh add, "Seriously, I'm going to focus on four key points that are noteworthy in this study."

When you face any problem, stay playful in the midst of the disaster and allow spontaneity to flourish – yours and that of your audience. Smile through the problems, and they will smile with you.

USE SELF-DEPRECATING
HUMOR AND SAVERS

"Laugh at yourself first, before anyone else can."

— Elsa Maxwell

Being able to laugh at oneself helps us let go of mistakes and bounce back to attack the problem anew. Everybody will "lay an egg" now and then. Even disasters can build increased enthusiasm when you control your response by using *prepared "Savers"* designed for the times your attempts at storytelling, participation, or humor fail.

Remember, audiences love to laugh along with people who can laugh at themselves. Even if one of your best stories gets nothing but confused stares, don't get stuck with "flop sweat" or go on as if nothing happened. Here's a collection of "savers" you can use when your humor doesn't work:

"I was going to talk about the myth of perfection, but I guess I've already taken care of that."

"Ladies & gentlemen. That was the humor portion of my meeting."

Look at your notes: "It says here 'Pause for laughter.'"

"Sometimes I speak on optimal performance – other days I can't even say it."

"Some of these I just do for me. Bear with me."

"I don't sing or dance. This is it!

VOICE CARE AND YOU

"Speakers cannot allow themselves the luxury of feeling tired, even when they are! The speaker's voice depends on an energetic body. In being assertive and enthusiastic, the abdominal muscles tighten and the rib cage expands. When tired, the opposite occurs and more breath is pushed through the vocal cords, straining them."

— Elizabeth Sabine

Speaking is more than moving lips; it involves the whole body to do it well. In effect, a good speaker has to stay in shape. When your body is in good shape, you can consistently give energy to your talk. Your voice will be more vibrant, alive and natural.

When speaking a lot, many speakers make the mistake of trying to protect their voice from overuse by speaking more softly. Not only will they not be as effective; they may very well strain their vocal chords worse than if they had remained more enthusiastic.

If you worry about using your voice in a forceful manner, watch a baby cry. A baby does not force wind through his voice box to get volume; a baby tightens his stomach muscles, opens his mouth and uses his body as his own boom box.

Rock singers have been taught this technique to sustain volume performance after performance. You don't have to cry like a baby or sing like a rock star. But your voice was made to be used with enthusiasm. Tighten those stomach muscles. Use it that way.

To build additional vocal confidence and clarity, sing. You can sing in your synagogue or church choir, in your car or in the shower . . . but sing. Singing will bring depth, amplitude and resonance to your speaking voice no matter what you speak about.

DO YOUR HOMEWORK —
LISTEN AND LEARN

"Transcribe your talk and read it. Then listen to an audi-otape of your speech and edit out anything that you can ask the question, 'Who cares?'"

— Patricia Fripp, CSP, CPAE

Don't be so enamored by the words coming out of your mouth that you forget to eliminate those that are not necessary. Few people are upset by presentations that end a little early.

By reading your transcribed messages instead of just listening to your own voice, you'll find it easier to eliminate unnecessary content, sharpen faulty grammar, and rework key phrasing.

While you're at it, you may find new and spontaneous stories, humor lines, or phrases that worked and can be refined and reused! Never leave such successes to chance, work on perfecting the content for future talks.

Don't forget to write down new material and impactful stories in a jour-nal or email "Keeper Log." The palest pencil mark is better than your best memory. Keep working and reworking your material to improve your presentations.

HANDLING EVALUATIONS,
THE BAD AND THE GOOD

"As speakers, let's view our evaluations as opportunities to improve and move on instead of reasons to beat ourselves up. Arrogance is expecting everyone to love us. Forgiveness is loving ourselves with flaws and imperfections."

— Barbara Sanfilippo, CSP

Everyone needs to be challenged to learn the art of future focused self-criticism. As a presenter make every error an opportunity to grow instead of an invitation for self-whipping. Life is like a moving vehicle with no brakes; if you spend too much time in the rearview mirror, you'll hit a tree out the front window.

When being self-critical, start by identifying what you did wrong and then focus on the future: What are you going to do to rectify the problem? How will you handle it next time? It's always easier to admit you made a mistake as a presenter than to admit you *are one!* Then get out of the rearview mirror and back into making the most of your day.

While you are at it, don't take your good performance for granted. After learning from your mistakes, end by catching yourself being effective in every presentation. Ask yourself: "What did I do today that I handled well? What worked for me today?" Write at least one successful accomplishment in your journal daily or send yourself and save an email that focuses on your successes.

Make sure some of your noted successes relate to your speaking skills. If you're not catching yourself being effective, you may be winning and not know it, because you're not keeping the right score.

GO TO SCHOOL WHEN
MAGIC HAPPENS

"In my passion, I do things. When something works, I remember it. I was making a point and was so intense about it, I smacked my chest and brought my other hand forward and saw the whole audience just about jump out of their chairs. I do it because it makes me feel good. I do it as an anchor for me that just puts me in a powerful passionate state."

— Tony Robbins

When something works, does it inspire you to make it happen again? If not, you are failing to understand a very important part about becoming the best speaker you can be. School is never out for the pro, and, sometimes, you are your own best teacher.

Every speaker knows that on certain platforms and with certain audiences, magic happens. The audience provides the energy and support and the speaker uses that energy to create what some would call a once-in-a-lifetime speech.

A pro wants to see that happen again and goes to school when magic happens! She listens to the tape. She takes notes on new lines or stories that worked. The first time magic happens it may truly have been magical, but from that moment forward you should never leave it to chance.

As Mark Twain used to say, "It takes me three weeks to prepare for an impromptu speech." Get busy working your "magic" into every presentation. By doing so, you will serve both yourself and your audience.

FLOP SWEAT CAN WORK FOR YOU

"One thing that's helped me is realizing that if I fail utterly, if I faint, babble, or spew, if people walk out flinging the heavy linen napkins onto the big round tables in disgust . . . my life continues as good as it was. Better. Because fewer people will ask me to speak. So flopping would be good for me. The minute I remember this I don't flop."

— Peggy Noonan

The freedom to fail is a powerful attitude adjuster. As speakers, the kiss of death is to get caught in the grip of *The Three P's — Perfection, Procrastination, Paralysis*. You become so afraid of doing the wrong thing, that you avoid saying what needs to be said, and become tongue-tied analyzing what to do about it!

It's often been said that if you can handle looking at the worst thing that can happen, you can free yourself to launch into just doing what you came to do. You've done the preparation. Even if you flop, life will go on for you and your audience.

But remember, the audience is ready to enjoy you. Move your feet and head for the lectern with the words of Yogi Berra spurring you forward: "When you come to the fork in the road, take it!" After all, when you can face the worst, you just may find that you experience the best — the joy of impacting an audience with *your* message! Seize the moment! Speak! Enjoy making a difference one more time!

SPEAKING RESOURCES . . .

Ailes, Roger with Kraushar, Jon. *You Are the Message*, Doubleday / Currency: 1995.

Antion, Tom. *Wake 'em Up: Business Presentations*, Anchor Publishing: 1999.

Boettinger, Henry M. *Moving Mountains: Or the Art and Craft of Letting Others See Things Your Way*, 1989.

Brody, Marjorie and Roddy, Miryam. *Speaking is an Audience-Centered Sport*, Career Skills Press: 2008.

Decker, Bert. *You've Got to Be Believed to Be Heard: The Complete Book of Speaking . . . In Business and in Life!* St. Martin's Press: 2008.

Detz, Joan. *It's Not What You Say, It's How You Say It*, St. Martin's Press: 2000.

DeVore, Kate & Cookman, Starr. *The Voice Book: Caring For, Protecting, and Improving Your Voice*, Chicago Review Press: 2009.

Frank, Milo. *How to Get Your Point Across in 30 Seconds or Less*, Pocket Books: 1986.

Gabrielle, Bruce. *Speaking PowerPoint: The New Language of Business*, Insights Publishing: 2010.

Glickstein, Lee. *Be Heard Now!* Broadway Books: 1998.

Grenville, Kleiser. *Successful Methods of Public Speaking*, The Project Gutenberg EBook, 2006.

Jeary, Tony. *Inspire Any Audience*, Trade Life Books: 2002.

Jeffreys, Michael. *Success Secrets of the Motivational Superstars: America's Greatest Speakers Reveal Their Secrets*, Prima Publishing: 1996.

Morgan, Nick. *Give Your Speech, Change the World: How To Move Your Audience to Action*, Harvard Business School Publishing: 2003.

Morrisey, George, Sechrest, T. and Warman, W. *Loud and Clear: How to Prepare and Deliver Effective Business and Technical Presentations*, Addison Wesley: 1997.

Osgood, Charles. *Osgood on Speaking: How to Think on Your Feet Without Falling on Your Face*, William Morrow: 1988.

Paulson, Terry. *Leadership Truths One Story at a Time*, Amber Eagle Press: 2006.

Paulson, Terry. *The Optimism Advantage: 50 Simple Truths to Transform Your Attitudes and Actions into Results*, Wiley: 2010.

Paulson, Terry L. *Making Humor Work: Take Your Job Seriously and Yourself Lightly*, Crisp Publications: 1989.

Pearce, Terry. *Leading Out Loud: Inspiring Change Through Authentic Communications*, New and Revised, John Wiley & Sons: 2003.

Pease, Barbara and Pease, Allan. *The Definitive Book of Body Language*, Bantam: 2006.

Pike, Robert W. *Creative Training Techniques Handbook: Tips, Tactics, and How-To's for Delivering Effective Training*, HRD Press: 2003.

Robertson, Jeanne. *Don't Let the Funny Stuff Get Away*, Rich Publishing: 1998.

Rye, David. *1,001 Ways to Inspire: Your Organization, Your Team and Yourself*, Career Press: 1999.

Silverman, Lori. *Wake Me Up When the Data Is Over: How Organizations Use Stories to Drive Results*, Jossey-Bass: 2006.

Sjodin, Terri. *Small Message, Big Impact: The Elevator Speech Effect*, Penguin/Portfolio: 2012.

Slutsky, Jeff and Aun, Michael. *The Toastmasters International Guide to Successful Speaking*, Dearborn Financial Publishing: 1997.

Valentine, Craig, Myerson, Mitch and Fripp, Patricia. *World Class Speaking: The Ultimate Guide to Presenting, Marketing and Profiting Like a Champion*, Morgan James: 2009.

Wacker, Mary and Silverman, Lori. *Stories Trainers Tell: 55 Ready-to-Use Stories to Make Training Stick*, Jossey-Bass: 2003.

Walters, Lilly. *Secrets of Successful Speakers: How You Can Motivate, Captivate, and Persuade*, McGraw-Hill: 1993.

Walters, Lilly. *What to Say When: A Complete Resource for Speakers, Trainers, and Executives*, McGraw Hill: 1995.

Weissman, Jerry. *Presenting to Win: The Art of Telling Your Story*, FT Press: 2008.

Weiss, Alan. *Money Talks: How to Make a Million As A Speaker*, McGraw-Hill: 1997.

ABOUT THE AUTHOR . . .

Dr. Terry Paulson is a Ph.D. psychologist, national columnist, honored professional speaker and author of the popular books, *The Optimism Advantage*, *They Shoot Managers Don't They*, *Leadership Truths One Story at a Time*, *Favorite Family Lectures*, and *Making Humor Work*.

His presentations help organizations, leaders, and teams leverage the optimism advantage and make change work! Since founding Paulson and Associates, Inc. in Agoura Hills, California, Dr. Paulson conducts practical and entertaining programs for companies such as Boeing, IBM, 3M, Johnson & Johnson, Merck, NASA, Nintendo, SONY, Starbucks, Wal-Mart, Warner Bros., and hundreds of hospitals, government agencies, and associations. His programs on effective communication and influencing up and across the organization have resulted in him being honored as one of only eight speakers to receive the Institute for Management Studies' Distinguished Faculty Designation.

Dr. Paulson is a Past President of both the National Speakers Association and the Global Speakers Federation. As an inductee into the CPAE Speakers Hall of Fame, he joins Ronald Reagan, Colin Powell and Norman Vincent Peale as a lifetime member, an honor given to fewer than 250 speakers worldwide since its inception in 1977. Terry's tasteful humor, practical programs, and down-to-earth style have earned him a deserved reputation as one of the nation's best keynote speakers. He brings knowledge, enthusiasm, and a refreshingly unique approach to every program he presents and every book he writes. *Business Digest* has called him "the Will Rogers of management consultants."

To learn more about Dr. Paulson's programs or to find more about some of his informative videos and books, visit www.terrypaulson.com.

9490601R00049

Made in the USA
San Bernardino, CA
18 March 2014